The Language of Canaan
and
The Grammar of Feminism

by

VERNARD ELLER

WILLIAM B. EERDMANS
PUBLISHING COMPANY
GRAND RAPIDS, MICHIGAN

Library of Congress Cataloging in Publication Data

Eller, Vernard.
  The language of Canaan and the grammar of feminism.

  1. Sexism in language.   2.   Bible — Language, style.
3.   Bible and feminism.   4.   Wittgenstein, Ludwig,
1889-1951.   I.   Title.
P120.S48E4   220.5′2   81-22193
ISBN 0-8028-1902-8   AACR2

To

KENNETH HAMILTON

*upon his retirement from
The University of Winnipeg
with deep personal appreciation.*

*Although my book and his
WORDS AND THE WORD
(Eerdmans 1971)
are in no way the same book,
they are in the same ballpark.*

Soli Deo Gloria

Contents

A Foreword

THIS book is bound to ruffle some feathers. In the calm before that happens, I would like to pin down a few ideas that perhaps we can hang on to when the going gets rough.

This book deals with just *one* topic, namely, "language"—which is why it is as brief as it is. But this means that you will not know where I stand on abortion, the Equal Rights Amendment, the ordination of women, homosexuality, the nature and extent of sexism, or even feminism per se. You will not know, because I will not be speaking about any of those things; I am speaking about language. And I would be grateful not to have readers jumping to conclusions for which they lack any evidence.

This book will make certain critical observations regarding the theological, anthropological, and philosophical bases underlying contemporary feminism. Yet I would submit that this in itself dare not be taken as grounds for calling me sexist, accusing me of sexism, or advancing any similar charge. Sexism (demeaning or denying the dignity of women) is a serious indictment to bring against anyone. It ought not to be bandied about, used in reference to whoever happens to disagree at some point with the feminist party-line.

Now, because I have chosen to address only the

one topic of "language," I admittedly do not give any close attention to or biblical documentation of a concept of "the feminine." That must await another and larger book. Yet, it will become apparent (1) that what I understand to be the scriptural ideal of "the feminine" is not the definition under which the feminist movement has chosen to operate. Nevertheless, (2) I do assert that scripture presents "the feminine" as the model and paradigm of the human race in its relation to the "masculinity" of God. Thus, essentially what it means to be "in the image of God" is to be feminine in respect to his masculinity.

Even clearer is the fact that the feminine represents *Israel's* stance toward her wooer God and *the church's* stance toward her bridegroom Christ. In consequence, then, the feminine is also a model for all humans (both male and female) in their relations to one another. So, although it is true that I disagree with the feminist idea of femininity, it does not at all follow that I am "antifeminine."

Unless, then, it is the case that only feminists are qualified to interpret scripture; that only feminists can tell us how language is structured, what it means, and how it functions; that only feminists (which is not even to say "women in general") are allowed to speak to the issue of what constitutes "the feminine"—unless the foregoing is the case, then my attempt on the subject is entirely in order. I am quite willing for critics to tell me I am "wrong" (particularly if they are willing to follow through and show me where I am wrong). But I trust they will be fair enough not to use glib accusations of "sexism" in putting down me and my work.

THE line of thought culminating in this book got its start through my reading of A. C. Thiselton's *Two Horizons,* an investigation of the hermeneutical implications of the work of several prominent philosophers. (Never mind what "hermeneutical" means; it makes no difference to the story.) One of the philosophers treated was Ludwig Wittgenstein. Thiselton got me interested; I read Wittgenstein himself; and in consequence, I was moved to write what you now hold.

Yet, after it was written, I had no idea what it was. I could tell that it was too long for an *article* and not long enough for a *book*—so what else is there? Not knowing what it was, the best I could see to do was to make xerox copies to mail around to friends and others who might be interested. Eventually, when it was actually accepted for publication, it was compared to what Will Strunk fondly called his "little" book, the Strunk/White *Elements of Style.*

That remark chased me back to a rereading of Strunk/White—something, I must confess, I had not done for several years. However, I soon discovered that these masters of language had said some things that were pertinent to my little book as well.

My circulation of the manuscript before it was known to be a book means that it received more prepublication feedback than is normally the case. Some of that merited response, and I have decided to do it here rather than mess up the original by trying to insert amendments and qualifiers in the requisite spots.

One critic opined that my analysis treats only the *English* Bible and would not apply in the same way to the original Hebrew or Greek. Neither he nor I know enough of those original languages to know what we were talking about; but the problem was easily solved with Strong's ancient but exhaustive concordance. For each occurrence of a given word in the English Bible (KJV), Strong includes a number key to indicate what was the Hebrew or Greek word it translates.

Thus we discover that all the different words spelled "m-a-n" in our soon-to-follow discussion of Genesis are simply spelled "-a-d-a-m" in the Hebrew. The one exception (which does not change the fact that 'adam is used both generically and as exclusive-masculine) is where Genesis 2:23-24 uses the word 'iysh (which is never anything except exclusive-masculine). So, if those verses were retranslated to read, "She shall be called Female, because she was taken out of Male. Therefore a male leaves his father and mother and cleaves to his wife," the English of the opening chapters of Genesis would be entirely congruent with the Hebrew.

The *Greek* is not particularly germane to our discussion, but the parallel between the original and the English translation holds in this case as well. *Anthropos* (which is translated "man") is used both as a generic (which is to say "sexually ignorant") and as exclusive-masculine. Any feminist accusations regarding the sexism of modern English have to take on the biblical languages at the same time.

A couple of respondents faced me with dictionary evidence that, contrary to my stated opinion, "*Everyone* should do *their* part" is correct usage. They quoted dictionaries to the effect that "their" can be taken as *singular*, the equivalent of "his or her." Yet, if this were indeed the case, writers and editors across the country would be using "their" in place of the awkward "his or her." They aren't, because they know that, at least among us, it is not acceptable usage. My guess is that the dictionaries have reference to what may have been a limited *British* usage. But Will Strunk says:

> *They.* Not to be used when the antecedent is a distributive expression such as *each, each one, everybody, every one, many a man.* Use the singular pronoun. . . . Similar to this, but with even less justification, is the use of the plural pronoun with the antecedent *anybody, any one, somebody, someone,* the intention being either to avoid the awkward "he or she," or to avoid committing oneself to either. (*Elements of Style,* p. 47)

In the book, I at one point argue that the word "persons" as a replacement for the customary "people" is a monstrosity, a moving away from a quite *personal* word to one that is tinged with the *impersonal.* I propose that the *proper* place to use "persons" is where the intent is to emphasize that they are strangers to one another. I even suggest that "persons" actually means "units" and would here go on to opine that "persons" is next door to that most impersonal of all "person words," namely, "*personnel.*" And now Strunk comes along with the one I hadn't seen, explaining *why* my feelings about that word are correct:

> The word *people* is best not used with words of number, in place of *persons.* If of "six people" five went away, how many "people" would be left? Answer: one people. (*Elements of Style,* p. 44)

As I say, "persons" is proper when you mean "units."

Early in this book, I speak of "flag words," i.e., innovative usages designed to call the reader's attention to the fact that the text is "feminist approved."

E. B. White (on p. 61 of *Elements of Style*) supports my point while speaking of an entirely different phenomenon. He cautions writers against introducing innovations into their text. The example he gives is spelling "through" as "thru." Rather than the reader being impressed that the author is a very smart and logical bird who is really improving the language, White suggests that the actual effect is to *distract* the reader, forcing him to pause in an effort at figuring out why things are not as they regularly are and expected to be. And certainly, the distraction is all the greater if the "figuring out" means becoming aware of a political cause that has absolutely nothing to do with the topic at hand.

FINALLY, I do want to express my gratitude to the readers of the not-yet-book who said that it really ought to be published. These include Bruce M. Metzger, Princeton Theological Seminary, and chairman of the NCC committee on the Revised Standard Version of the Bible; Thomas H. Middleton, writer of the regular "Language" feature in *Saturday Review;* and Anthony C. Thiselton, University of Sheffield (England), author of *Two Horizons* and himself Ludwig Wittgenstein's *Fürsprech*.

The support of these experts makes me much more confident of my position and of the fact that what we have here actually is *a book*. And so, to the feather ruffling.

CHAPTER ONE

The Teachers and the Taught

IT WAS, I think, Karl Barth who once said something to the effect that Christians have an obligation to become competent in "the language of Canaan" (i.e., biblical ways of thinking and speaking) rather than simply demanding that everything be translated into *our* language (i.e., contemporary forms of thought).

More recently I have learned—largely from Paul Holmer's *The Grammar of Faith*—that "grammar" now is the key by which theology is to be done. I may have come late and through the back door, but I finally am on board (and that is not a mixed metaphor; boats do have doors, I believe).

It was, then, from Douglas Hofstadter's not at all theological book, *Godel, Escher, and Bach*, that I got excited about the idea of different "levels"—of meaning, thought, language, discourse, conceptualization, analysis. The concept is a perfectly obvious one, one with which we all are well familiar in one way or another, one I myself have used to good effect under some such terminology as "context," "perspective," "world view," "horizon." Yet never before had the idea struck me as so clear, compelling, and pregnant.

Then I discovered that Ludwig Wittgenstein was the true developer of this way of thinking. His "language games" *are* "levels"—or perhaps more precisely put, his language games are "the linguistic hardware we use in dealing with a particular level of meaning." And his "grammar" is perhaps "the software principles and rules that govern the use of the hardware for that particular level." In any case, it is Barth, Holmer, Hofstadter, and Wittgenstein who led me to undertake this linguistic adventure.

CHAPTER TWO

Temperature Levels

As the current feminist grammar was introduced and urged upon us, my first and continuing reaction was, "That sure does make hash of English rhetoric!" The feminizing of scripture, hymns, poetry, sermon, and liturgy frequently produces aesthetic monstrosity. And some usages—such as the ground-gaining "everyone should do *their* part"—are just plain wrong. Now I know that this *aesthetic* loss is usually considered an insignificant price to pay for the *political* gain involved. But as a writer who feels strongly that being beautiful and communicating beauty is an absolutely essential function of language, I inevitably have had questions worded around "birthrights" and "messes of pottage."

My second *level* of realization (you might as well be learning how "levels" operate) was that, although the feminist grammar surely is not deliberately antirhetorical, it is most deliberately *political*. Its linguistic innovations (such as "chairperson," "humankind," "God gives us God's grace," "he or she") are code symbols, each a little red flag bearing the letters FA (Feminist Approved). And the game—the language game—is to score points by the amount of writing that can be labeled FA. "Look: Eller has conceded! Or, if not

3

that, at least an editor has *dragged* him in. Either way, you can chalk up another one for us."

The positive harm in this business is that it obstructs my efforts in writing. I have to be free to talk about feminism when I choose to and free not even to think about feminism while I am trying to talk about something else. Yet just when my reader and I are finally getting our heads together—just when I'm working hardest to keep my language so right and unobtrusive that the reader won't even notice he's reading *language* but simply be thinking the *thought* along with me—just then some meddling editor sticks in an FA flag and blows my whole attempt.

My reader is *distracted*, and responds in one of two ways. He could say: "Oh! Feminism! Gee, for a moment I had almost forgotten that there even are two different varieties of human beings. Can't let that happen; we want always to be *inclusive*. Men *and* women. Women *and* men. Got it." The other response is: "Oh, Vernard, an FA flag! When did you start this? I would never have thought it of you. Are you letting those feminists push you around?"

Either way, I've lost the reader's close attention and he my train of thought. Getting people to think is not easy at best; and I do resent outsiders interrupting my class in order to mount a flag parade for their political cause. (Notice that I object only to *my* prose being used this way against my wishes. I have no objection at all to the writer who *wants* to do a flag parade.)

As my third level of realization, I immediately saw that the effort to move our God-language *beyond gender* has profound implications regarding theology and the authority of scripture—implications to which no one seemed to be giving attention.

4

MORE recently, then, as a fourth level—the Wittgenstein level—I have come to see that, not only the God-language, but the entire feminist grammar has important theological repercussions. So let us turn our attention to the linguistic anthropology of feminist grammar. (And by the way, as we proceed to designate different levels as being "higher" or "lower," it will become apparent that the levels just described are numbered in the reverse of customary usage. My realization developed from lower levels toward higher ones. But from here on, No. 1 will denote the *highest* level and so on down.)

CHAPTER THREE

Water Level

ALLOW me to set the terms of our thought with a paradigm—an entirely neutral and nonthreatening example to which we then can regularly refer as we move into the matter itself. Our category is WATER; and the word which is operative on the highest language-game level, No. 1, is "water."

Now the distinction between a high level and lower levels is not at all that of "truth"—or even degrees of being "truer." No, as long as the language is being used correctly, each level is equally "true." It is, rather, that a high-level language has far broader applicability, is much more useful within human discourse, and can say so many more things than can a low-level language.

And because the word "water" treats water as *simple* (as opposed to complex), as an *integer*, as a homogeneity based upon the commonality found throughout its many and varied manifestations, the uses of the word are endless. It can be applied to everything from teardrops to Pacific Oceans. It is useful in getting yourself a drink: "Bring me a glass of *water*, please!" (although, for the sentence to succeed, the word "please" may be just as operative as "water"). It can be used to romanticize: "moonlit water." "Dirty water," on the other hand, evokes very different images. The word can provide us with what is probably the most evocative one-word description of a planet: "waterless." It can be used to make the crucial but undefinable distinction between "milky water" and "watery milk." It can even help make the absolute distinction between "water" and "milk"—although technically, I guess, milk is nothing more than a particular type of polluted water. Yet the language knows which mixtures are to be called "dirty water" and which are not. In truth, because of its inclusive, homogenous reference, the word "water" belongs to a very high-level language game, notable for its power in identifying and handling *particularities*. (Wittgenstein is explicit in saying that the *power* of a grammar lies in its potential for handling *particulars*, rather than in what it can do with abstractions and generalities.)

ON the second level (actually it should be named Level 3, because I intend to insert another Level 2 in just a bit), WATER is approached through the word (or formula) "H_2O." Notice that this way is just as "true" as is calling the stuff "water"—yet this is an entirely different approach and a very much "weaker" one. Now, rather than treating water as a homogeneity, it is defined in terms of its constituents, namely, hydrogen atoms and oxygen atoms. Water here is seen as a mixture (or better yet, a combination) of the two varieties of atoms.

Now there may be a strictly logical and scientific argument claiming that the "H_2O Approach" cuts in at a level prior to the "Water Approach," in that, in order for them to combine as water, hydrogen and oxygen atoms had first to exist as separate entities. (Whether this is so or not, it sounds as though it *should* be.) But no matter; from the standpoint of human experience, the priority is clearly the other way around. And again, it was Wittgenstein who argued that language is always the product and vehicle of "human experience" rather than anything else. The race knew "water" for untold millenia before it discovered "H_2O"; millions of people yet today are totally competent dealers in "water" without even knowing that it is "H_2O"; most of us who do "know" still have never experienced water as hydrogen and oxygen; and even that scientist who is most H_2O-minded still spends by far the greater part of his water-life in the "water" language game rather than the "H_2O" one.

It is humbling to think of all the things you can't say in H_2O language. My guess is that you have to translate "H_2O" back up to "water" even to *think* of its wetness, its thirst-quenchingness, its drowning-ability, its fire-inhibitingness, or whatever other properties it suggests. Certainly the term "H_2O" does not hold out much in the way of romantic possibilities. And you can't even say "dirty water" in this language. That a given H_2O molecule could be "dirty" is an impossible concept (I think). And water, now, can be described only as a collection of (clean) H_2O molecules. So the best we can say (or think) is "clean water-molecules in congregation with a large number of foreign molecules." Yet, if I may say so, that "word" cannot begin to support either the aesthetic, emotive, culinary, or passionate overtones that can be communicated with "dirty water." It would be next to impossible to write poetry without the word "water." So, although for certain specialized purposes it is virtually essential to speak of and deal with water as being H_2O, this still represents a very weak and low level of language compared to the glorious word "water." The two words may be synonyms, but they sure are a long way from being *synonymous*.

I think there is at least one level of discourse that lies between "water" and "H_2O." Almost invariably, close thought will reveal the possiblity of more language levels than are first apparent. This is because we truly are dealing with levels of human thought and language rather than with anything inherent in the objective reality itself. Water neither knows nor cares whether it is water, collected droplets, massed molecules, or something else.

Yet it is quite possible to *think* of water (all water) as consisting essentially of Level-2 "collected droplets"—and this without necessarily demanding or implying the next move to Level-3 "molecules." It probably is true that every bit of water on earth has at one time or another existed as a droplet which was then collected into its respective puddle. At least the Psalmist writes:

> Little drops of water,
> Little grains of sand,
> Make the mighty ocean
> And the pleasant land.

(What do you mean? I can't help it if *you* didn't learn your memory verses when you were a kid!) Yet here is a language level that is so little needed or contributive that we have not even developed the language to operate it.

JUST so, there are language levels *below* Level-3 "H_2O." Water, at Level 4, *could* be thought of as consisting in a complex configuration, not of atoms, but of electrons, protons, and neutrons. And because scientists are discovering that even these particles are made up of yet smaller ones, lower language levels will keep multiplying as long as science keeps turning up the stuff with which to do them. Any and all such levels do, of course, constitute accurate and true descriptions of water. It may even be useful at times to approach water from one of these levels. Yet the language here is very limited and weak; it has to be invented as we go along and likely will never become a part of normal discourse.

Notice that there are any number of class words ("river," for example) that do not even figure into our scheme, because they are not intended to refer to any and all water. Consequently, "river" does not represent a language level of the category WATER.

To you, our "water treatment" probably has not seemed *theological* at all. Yet it is far from irrelevant. As we now turn to theologizing proper, reference to this water model will help things along considerably.

CHAPTER FOUR

Top-Level Man

FOR this run-through, our category is MAN. As "water" was itself the Level-1 *word* for the category WATER, so here the Level-1 word likewise is "man." (The interesting problem is that neither the category nor its Level-1 word can be defined without going to a lower language level to do so—which means that the synonym will always be somewhat inadequate to that which it would define. But, being aware of that situation, let us rather call our category THE HUMAN RACE.)

The one and only Level-1 word is "man"—with the pronouns "he," "him," and "his."

So God created *man* in his own image,
in the image of God he created *him*.

(Gen. 1:27)

To say that this is a Level-1 word is to assert that, in its language game, it can say things and express truths for which no other language level is adequate. In the present case, the advantages are these: "Man" treats the race as *simple* (not complex), as a totality, an integer, a homogeneity. The word is not a *collective*; its pronouns are *singular*. The totality "man" is not achieved by adding up constituent individuals—any more than the word "water" implies an adding up of droplets or of hydrogen and oxygen atoms. Indeed, the very purpose behind the word "man" is to enable us to say that the race as such, in its essential unity, is both prior to and superior to any and all component analysis or individuation (whether of gender, ethnic grouping, discrete individuals, or any other subdivision). This word enables scripture to say that God created "man" *before* he created any of man's component particulars, that any person's essential identity lies in being "man" before being anything else—even before being "a person" ("in my own right," as contemporary thought so wrongheadedly adds).

Now there are other words that can go this far—or at least would seem to point to this understanding. However, "man" takes one further giant step of which I know no other word to be capable. Not only are its pronouns *singular*, they are *personal*. "In the image of God he created *him* [not *it*]." "Man" is, at one and the same time, total, singular (simple), and *personal*. In this Level-1 language game, there is no possibility of adding up *personal* integers (individual human beings) and getting an *impersonal* total—even though the language of every other level can do nothing else. In fact, Level-1 language can't even perform such a computation, because it has no knowledge that the race even *has* components. When it calls "man" *personal*, it is *not* referring to the "personality" of *individuals*.

Yet the total "man" *is* personal ("man, *him*"). The race itself is to be treated as if it were a single person. (That last sentence is a very poor one indeed. Because it is an attempt to use Level-2 language in making a Level-1 statement, it cannot be other than grossly misleading. With the pronouns "itself" and "it," that sentence assumes that "the race" actually is *impersonal* but that we are to practice the "as if" fiction of thinking of it as personal. That is the best Level 2 can do; but it is not all what Level 1 has in mind. You can't do one level of thinking in the language of another level, because—as per Wittgenstein—language and thought are not two different things but two different descriptions of the same thing.)

I'M sorry; I have no other option than to use the word "man" in explaining what "man" means. But man is to be thought of as *personal*, as *a person*, because, in a wholly accurate sense, he (not "it") *is* a person—there is no fiction involved. Scripture simply *has* to have access to this level of language, because it is totally committed to saying that God not only relates himself to individual humans but also to the race as such. And the God/race relationship is just as truly person-to-person as is the God/individual one. In fact, the God/race relationship is the prior, paradigmatic model of what "personhood" means. "God created *man* in his own image." It is not said that God created a bunch of individuals who got together and formed a corporation named MAN. And notice that it is this person, *man*, who was created in the image of God. We have assumed otherwise, but scripture does not say that each individual human being is in the image of God; no, man as a whole is.

The person "man," I would suggest, is better equipped to "image" God than any individual is—partly because the corporate (community) nature of his being already has him more correspondent to God than any individual could be. And thus, in imaging God, "man" also can manifest a truer personhood, a more Godlike approximation of what it means to be "a person," than can any human individual. Indeed, the implication of scripture seems to be that the only hope of an individual's becoming a true "person" is through his participation in the fuller personhood of "man."

NOW I am quite aware that this biblical way of thinking is diametrically opposed to contemporary fashion. There our language levels would have to take a reverse order. The given datum, the starting point, the factual basis of personhood is now *the individual's* self-identity ("I am somebody"/"I am a person in my own right"/"I am a woman"/"I am black"). And if *this* is the source and center of personhood, then suggestions of any superior personhood must be suppressed or reinterpreted. Thus, the explanation is that primitive and unsophisticated cultures came up with the quaint idea of *projecting* individual human personhood back onto the race as a whole (as they did it forward onto their pet animals). Likewise, they anthropomorphized their idea of "God," making "him" not only a "person" in their own image but—quaintest of all—a "masculine" person at that.

So goes the contemporary understanding of "personhood." But the one point I wish to make here is that the Bible has that course of personhood just the opposite: *from* God the Father (the ultimate paradigm of all personhood), *through* his creating of "man" in his own image, *to* individual personhood derived from one's participation in the personhood of "man." Nevertheless, contemporary thought (both feminist and otherwise) finds normative personhood only in the human individual and understands all else as a projection from there. And this anthropological switch—showing up most clearly as a reversal of lan-

14

guage levels—is, I contend, responsible for throwing modern theology clear outside its biblical parameters.

AN EXCURSUS ON THE "REPRESENTATIVE INDIVIDUAL"

THE Bible's Level-1 use of "man" as a term of total, singular (simple), personal reference can be understood as one specimen of the literary device that treats a *group* as if it were a single, representative *individual* ("The Christian believes . . ."/"The student will . . ."/"My reader knows . . ."). Such usages do not belong in our present scheme, because they have no intention of referring to the entire race. Also, as we have suggested, "man" is not as fictitiously "a person" as is true with these other instances. Yet, whatever the case with "man," this representative individual device is one of the strengths of our language, enabling us easily to say (and thus think) many things that we could not say (or could say only with great difficulty) otherwise.

For example, when I write "*The Christian* stakes his life thus-and-so," this is not at all the same thing as writing "*Christians* stake their lives thus-and-so." In the first case I am saying that the ideal, prototypical individual, model of the historic faith, *would* act thus-and-so. However, in the second case it would be to say that the mass of flesh-and-blood people who call themselves Christians *do* act in a certain way. And the trouble with that one is that it so often is simply not true. Yet whenever I *do* want to make the latter statement, the language affords me a way of doing so.

And I *insist* on the right to address my readers as "my reader" rather than "my readers." All of my writing is carefully designed as one-on-one converse. Be my readers ever so many (and may their tribe increase), yet, with me at the typewriter and they at the resultant page, it is you and me, we two and no more. The last thing I would ever think of doing is addressing that mob of thousands upon thousands (with some of my stuff, yes!). In fact, even to *think* of that mob would immediately paralyze me from writing a word. "My reader" is an idea totally different from "my readers." "My readers" are a statistic; "my reader" is a person.

The Bible, of course, could not even gets its message off the ground without using this representative individual device—largely, I suppose, because of its profound commitment to the "man" anthropology. Yet even those who consider "Adam" to have been a historical individual must also be ready to see him as a representational figure if the biblical account is to have any real significance. Israel (the people) is frequently described as an individual—sometimes a male and very often a female. In the New Testament, the church regularly is treated as a female individual. And Isaiah wants to talk about "the Assyrian, the rod of [God's] anger"—and it is self-evident why this figure should be male.

Quite apart from the power of this device in saying what wants to be said, undoubtedly the Bible also uses it to underline its own understanding of the nature and importance of *community*. Often, these representational figures are as much challenges to an ideal as they are descriptions of what actually obtains.

The language, note well, through its pronouns, has the power to present the representative person as being of either gender. Yet, obviously, that gender designation has nothing at all to do with the gender of the group's constituents; its function, rather, is as a means of characterizing *the corporation as a whole*—and usually in relation to some other entity (gender itself and all gender language is necessarily *relational* in character). Thus, the church is to be feminine in relation to what? To the masculinity of God (or Christ), of course. And the relationship is just as essential the other way around: the masculinity of God has no meaning at all unless there is a femininity toward which it can act "masculinely." (And "the Assyrian," by the way, is masculine in relation to the Jerusalem he is ready to rape.)

AN EXCURSUS ON THE ALLEGED SEXISM OF CERTAIN WORDS

NOW the current feminist grammar would prohibit both of the language-game possibilities we have just described. Regarding Level-1 anthropology, the problem, of course, is that the key word is spelled "m-a-n" with pronouns spelled "h-e," "h-i-m," and "h-i-s." Regarding the representative individual device, the problem is only with cases that call for "bad" pronouns. Yet we are left with no option but to drop these language games entirely. There is no Level-1 synonym for "man"; it is either use that word or go to lower levels of discourse. Regarding the representative individual, the standard ploy is to change the reference to *plural* ("The Assyrian is . . ." to "The Assyrians are . . ."). This, of course, is to desert the device entirely and to lose all of its distinctive power. Another move is to retain the singular but *double* the pronouns ("he or she" and the like). Yet this way, too, is entirely to desert the device. The reference is no longer to a single, representational figure but to any one actual constituent of the group, some *particular* member who, of course, is either male or female.

17

Wittgenstein, however, could have showed us that the entire dilemma is unnecessary. He tells us that words are not what they are commonly understood to be, namely discrete, hard-shelled nuggets of meaning. Words do not *have* meaning; they *gain* meaning from the use to which they are put. They are "meaningful" only as part of a larger context of sentence, paragraph, and even the life situations of speaker and hearer. A word's only "meaning" lies in its *function;* its spelling, etymology, history, et al., are as irrelevant as its length or typeface. Thus it is inconceivable that any particular word *could* be "sexist"; it is only that the word can be *used* for a sexist purpose, to say something of sexist intent—which, of course, is just as true for any number of words the feminists approve as it is for those they reject.

But if I were to give you, say, simply the word "bridge," until I put the word to some use you couldn't even tell whether I was talking about "a structure spanning a hiatus," "a card game," "a dental piece," "the command to arch your back," or some other meaning of those five letters. And until it is put to some use, neither can you know that any word spelled "m-a-n" (or embodying that configuration of letters) *has* to carry or intend "masculine" implications.

I could write: "He was under the bridge, flat on his back, playing bridge, when his buddy cried, 'Bridge!' He did; and the bridge popped out of his mouth and landed on the bridge of his nose."

Now under the theory that words of a particular *spelling must* be tied to a particular *meaning*, that passage would have to represent gross confusion. Plainly, it does not. Just that much, and I have communicated a mouthful. Here you can spot five different words, each spelled "b-r-i-d-g-e," yet none depending upon a knowledge of any of the others. Yet, without half trying, you can know for a certainty which is which and what is the function of each. And I didn't have to give you any definitions, either. All it took was a bit of context (actually, very little of that): "under" in the first instance; "playing" in the second; "he did" in the third; "mouth" in the fourth; and "nose" in the fifth.

If my passage had been not quite so overdone and had occurred in a normal reading context, you probably would race through a series of "same-spelled words" without even realizing that you had accomplished a minor miracle of interpretation. Actually, the context in which you are reading has you operating in a portion of the brain where you aren't even aware that there *are* definitions of "bridge" other than the one you want. So the suggestion that any word of a particular spelling invariably carries tinges of a particular meaning is very wide the truth of the matter.

WITHIN our larger discussion, we are going to spot words spelled "m-a-n" on three different language levels and at least once entirely outside our scheme. The words range from sexually ignorant (undifferentiating) through sexually inclusive to sexually exclusive. But there are no grounds for arguing that, because they are all *spelled* the same, they must all *be* the same word or that the overtones of one must necessarily color all. The *function* of each is plainly different; and the function *is* the word.

And how can we be so positive regarding "man" (and the "he, him, his" pronouns)? By three thousand years of field testing, that's how. Looking at nothing

19

more than the opening chapters of Genesis—from the Hebrew original through many different languages (including New Testament Greek and English)—the different same-spelled "man" words have functioned perfectly, communicating their various thoughts without a hitch to countless generations of both the learned and the unlearned. Modern feminists can, if they wish, say, "We have *chosen* not to understand the language according to its established grammar." They cannot claim that the grammar itself no longer functions as it should.

Of course I know that the feminist attack was intended to target only the "man" words themselves, not to eliminate Level-1 discourse or the representative-individual device. However, we see here a phenomenon we will run into time and time again: the "accidental" side effects of the grammar change regularly turn out to support the basic philosophy of which feminism is a part. Wittgenstein could have told us: tamper with the grammar of a language and you are shifting its basic world view at the same time. "Language" fixes parameters for "thought" just as much as "thought" creates "language."

The broad world view of our day—of which feminism is but one expression—tends to focus almost exclusively upon the personhood of the individual, and to resist anything that would suggest its subordination. This is what Christopher Lasch has in mind in speaking of "the culture of narcissism." One of its most revealing mottoes is a book title that recently caught my eye: *I Exist, I Need, I'm Entitled.* To eliminate the language-level that has enabled us to speak of the superior personhood of the race (or of God) and to squelch the community implications of the representative individual device—all of this clearly serves the interests of the regnant philosophy. But just as clearly, it is utterly impossible to do *biblical theology* without these linguistic means.

CHAPTER FIVE

I'll Level With You

THE Hebrew parallelism of Genesis 1:27 is an intriguing one. The first line reads: "So God created man in
his own image, in the image of God he created him."
That line we already have seen to be a paradigm of
Level-1 anthropological discourse. The line itself includes a doubling—probably as a means of emphasiz-
ing its priority. Yet the second, antiphonal line (which
normally functions as a parallel, a repetition of the
first line's idea) in this case reads: "Male and female he
created *them*."

Although referring to the same creation of the same
subject, the antiphon uses a plural pronoun where the
phon (if that's the word I want) had used a singular
one. We seem to have a contradiction and/or a
grammatical error. For instance, when we find written, "Everyone should do their part," it *is* an error,
although not because it is wrong to refer to a human
grouping in the plural. The error comes when, in one
and the same statement, the sentence tries to operate
on two different language levels. When the antecedent
is identifying the group as singular, the pronoun dare
not call it plural. But Genesis 1:27 does not have this
problem. It consists of two *different* (although very
similar) statements, each of which functions properly
on its own language level. Thus it is a repetition which

is much more than just a repetition. Each of the two statements is equally true; no one is being forced to decide whether the race actually *is* singular or whether it is plural. Indeed, the full truth is all the fuller for being able to include both statements; the truth-seeker is more truth-finding for being able to converse on both (on all) language levels.

Yet it becomes plain that "male and female" should not be taken to represent Level 2; there are other levels that come in between. Let's take time to get them in the picture.

LEVEL 2: The key terms here are: "the human race," "humanity," "mankind," "humankind" (this last being a flag word, invented to escape the gender implications of "mankind," which, functionally, had no gender implications to begin with).

As with Level 1, each of these words is *total* in reference and *singular* (simple) in treating the race as an integer. But the difference now is that Level 2 sees the race as *impersonal* rather than as a person; each of our words calls for the pronoun "it." We are not implying that this language level is in any way improper or unnecessary. In many contexts, impersonally is the only accurate way to describe the race—even though there are also many true things that can be said on Level 1 that simply are not possible to Level 2. (By the way, this Level 2 is the equivalent of WATER's Level-1 "water." Because there would be no particular truth function involved, WATER does not want the possibility of being spoken of as a person.)

An interesting speculation is whether any of the terms on Level 2 is actually a *collective*. It is quite possible to arrive at a total by adding up parts and yet treat that resultant as though you had created a *singular* (an integer). If we do have a collective, "mankind" would be the most likely suspect. Yet it seems right that even this word should be understood as being derived downward from Level-1 "man as a whole" rather than upward from a lower level, "man as a human individual." It is probably correct that—with Level-2 "mankind," as with Level-1 "water"—the language does not betray (actually, cannot betray) even the possibility of analyzing the race into components.

There is one term that might appear to belong here (if not on Level 1) but which, instead, falls clear outside our scheme. The term simply is not used the way it looks as though it should be. "Everyone/everybody" would appear to be *total* (but is not), is *singular* (calling for singular pronouns), and is *personal* (personal pronouns). Yet, at best, the word denotes "people in general" rather than "the totality of people." And more precisely, it is a synonym of "anyone" or "whoever"— thus signifying "any person chosen at random" rather than a grouping of any sort. "Everyone" is in no way *total*; and even its *singularity* and *person reference* apply to that random individual rather than to the character of the race.

LEVEL 3: At this point we are going to complicate matters by speaking of Level 3+: "people"; Level 3: "man (plural), men"; and Level 3−: "persons." With the exception of "man (plural)," these terms normally function with the adjective "all" ("all people," "all men," etc.). Each term, of course, calls for personal pronouns. This level has distinguished itself from Level 2 by leaving behind both the *singular* race and the *impersonal* one. Level 3 corresponds to the "droplet" level of WATER and is marked by the discovery that the race can be approached by analyzing it into its constituents, namely, human individuals. Each of the words is *plural*, and each is a *collective*.

The word "people" ("all people") is a unique case—and unique in a way that qualifies it for a plus sign. "People" is *plural* but plural with a difference. It is not constructed over a singular by giving one a plural ending or form. One "person" plus another "person" equals "persons." But what equals "people"? One "peep" plus another "peep"? "People" does have a singular, namely "a people." Yet, although the plural is a collective (of "peeps"), the singular does not refer to a constituent individual but to a *community*. "All people" manages to refer to the race collectively but without accentuating the individuality of that which is collected—and thus it stands a notch above the rest of Level 3.

With "persons" ("all persons")—in addition to being rhetorically "blah!"—the movement is in precisely the opposite direction. The word obviously is constructed by giving the singular a plural ending—which has the effect of keeping each "droplet" individual. "Persons" may get collected; but they do very little combining. And this linguistic feature is, of course, further emphasized by the contemporary philosophical overtones of "person"—namely autonomy, self-containedness, liberation, resistance to subordination. In consequence, "persons" speaks of the most loosely knit collective possible, a passel of *strangers*.

It must be said that this "stranger" aspect of the word "persons" does have its proper function. That is why the newspaper report tells us that seventeen *persons* (read: "units") were killed in a certain disaster. We are being told that the only thing those individuals had in common was that they chanced to die at the same time—a very loose collective indeed. Consequently, I have been completely unable to figure the rationale for the switch to "persons" where the word "people" had been serving very well. Certainly no considerations of *sexism* are involved. Yet "persons" clearly is a flag word of mod-speak (and perhaps of mod-church-speak in particular). But I do not understand why, in a worship litany, the congregation should be called "persons" when they are "people"—perhaps even people on the way to becoming "a people." No, "all persons" is definitely Level 3−. And again, linguistic "accident"(?) has the effect of skewing our discourse away from its biblical parameters.

Back, then, to Level 3 (straight). It is intriguing to discover that, in Genesis 1:26 (the verse immediately preceding the one we have been addressing), the text reads: "Then God said, 'Let us make man in our image . . . and let *them* have dominion. . . .'"

Here is a "man" that is *collective;* the collected sum is given a *plural* pronoun. Thus, although both are spelled "m-a-n," this is not at all the same word as the "man" of the succeeding verse. There, recall, rather than being a collective, "man" was an integer of such integrity that there was no hint of even the possibility of addressing "him" in terms of component individuals. Although spelled the same and appearing in consecutive verses, the two words *function* differently enough to make it apparent that they are in no way the *same* word.

It needs to be noted, also, that the component analysis of Level-3 "man" is not that of Level-4 "male and female" (even though both come within verses

26–27). The "them" of verse 26 recognizes a plurality of human individuals without suspecting that they can be separated into two different categories; only the "them" of verse 27 finally discovers that there are both male individuals and female individuals. It turns out that the biblical writers were most adept at playing WITTGENSTEIN long before Ludwig even invented the game.

Actually, Level-3 "man" is a rather rare usage. Its partner "men" ("all men") is much more common— even as it displays a construction that is more common to this level. "Man" may imply a somewhat tighter collective than does "all men"—in that it *looks* like a singular and does not require the assistance of the adjective "all." Nevertheless, "people" is the most powerful word on this level and probably the one most frequently used.

(Notice that on none of these three levels can either "man" or "men" have any sort of gender implication. On these levels there is as yet no knowledge of gender and no means of expressing such. And it is essential to purposes of human discourse to be able to speak of the race without dragging gender into the conversation.)

LEVEL 4: "Male and female [read also: "man and woman" or "men and women"] he created them."

This language level is *biblical*; it is *true*; it is *essential* to a full-truth anthropology—there are no questions on that score. This is the equivalent of the H_2O level regarding WATER. As it was there discovered that water could be described in terms of its atomic constituents (hydrogen atoms and oxygen atoms), here it is discovered that humanity can be described in terms of its constituent male atoms and female atoms. Yet there is a difference—or at least the possibility of a difference.

The H_2O game and the Bible game are both very much committed to *molecular* theory. Water is not just a mixture of hydrogen and oxygen atoms; it is a proper *bonding* of those atoms into molecules.

The Bible has it: "Therefore a man leaves his father and his mother and cleaves to his wife, and they become one [molecule]" (Gen. 2:24).

(And here, by the way, where for the first time we have said "*a* man," we have a new "m-a-n" word which is entirely different from what we have seen heretofore. By itself it identifies just one gender and thus cannot denote the totality of the race. It falls entirely outside our scheme.)

But notice that the biblical thought is molecular throughout. We did not start with an independent "man-atom" which then, along with a "woman-atom," decided to form a molecule. No, the "man-atom" left his "parents-children molecule" in order to form a "husband-wife molecule"—which itself in time became another "parents-children molecule." Scripture knows nothing of a theory that makes atomic existence normative, with the atoms exercising the freedom to form molecules only if and when they promise to give atomic satisfaction, and the freedom to dissolve molecules whenever they fail to satisfy. Rather, "the Lord God said 'It is not good that the [atom] should be alone'" (Gen. 2:18); and he proceeded to get his creation "right" by thoroughly molecularizing it.

THUS, the Bible. Yet the custom of our day is to read "Male and female he created them" in terms of "atomic physiques," i.e., the priority and independence of atoms—and this, apparently, out of hatred for the mutual subordination necessarily involved in molecular existence.

Plainly, it is here on Level 4 that the feminist grammar centers in—to the detriment of any higher levels of discourse and to the actual exclusion of Level 1. But the feminists are not alone in this, for the very tendency of our world is toward an atomistic anthropology: "I am a woman"/"I am black"/"I am a person in my own right" . . . this rather than "No man is an island." And such a philosophy as much as demands that Level 4 be the primary language-game.

The basic principle of this grammar is *inclusiveness*—and feminist terminology has that word just exactly right. But consider what the term means: it means being careful to name every single constituent, so that not one is excluded from the end result. Miss one and the language now is "exclusive" rather than "inclusive." Yes, it is true that none of our higher-level games was *inclusive* (in this sense); yet none of them was *exclusive*, either. They *couldn't* be. Because they didn't even recognize that the total integer consists of components, they didn't have the language that could exclude any. (Level 3 did recognize components—yet all of one sort, namely, human beings—and so still didn't have the language that could exclude any.) You can't be "sexist" on Levels 1–3, because there sex doesn't even exist. Rather than "inclusive," these levels would have to be characterized as "sexually ignorant, or nondifferentiating."

Now if the important thing is that our language be "nonexcluding," these higher levels are the safe and sure way to go. But go the way of Level-4 inclusiveness, and there will always be questions: Does "men and women" do justice to the *children* in our midst? Does "male and female" properly include our eunuchs, transsexuals, transvestites, bisexuals, and homosexuals? Have we overlooked anyone? And as with H_2O, when we go to still lower language levels, the list of components invariably lengthens. Thus, if we choose what we might as well call Level 5, an old Sunday school song represents the big try:

Red and yellow, black and white—
They are precious in his sight.
Jesus loves the little children of the world.

But will just four colors add up to "all"? How about the gray children that are always underfoot—or the mottled ones? And does the song mean to imply that Jesus doesn't love *big* kids? Try the inclusive method of writing, and the nitpickers will get you every time.

NOW the Bible, operating out of a *high-level anthropology* in the interests of a *human being theology* (and thus, I would think, not particularly excited about black theology, feminist theology, and other exclusivist theologies), tends generally to use sexually ignorant terms. Speaking only for myself, in by far the greater part of what I write, I want to be as sexually ignorant as possible. At the typewriter, I am willing to forget what sex I am. Nor am I interested in knowing the sexual status of my reader; that shouldn't make any difference at all to the hearing of what I have to say. When, for instance, I talk about "the Christian" who believes this or that, I don't want readers trying to guess whether he is male or female. At this language level we don't even know what sex is. He (the Christian) is a representative personification of the entire Christian community and nothing else. (And those pronouns do not change the case one iota. They are part of the same language level as their antecedents; and if the antecedents are sexually ignorant, so are the pronouns.) I use the upper language levels precisely because there is no way they can be excluding of a gender group or of any other human constituency. They *can* speak—have the words to speak—only of human beings as such or of the race as a whole.

But what happens? I write: "The Christian must find his role in society"—a perfectly correct, sexually ignorant sentence. There comes along a copyeditor with a Level-4 fixation and changes it to "The Christian must find his or her role in society."

"What did you do to my sentence?" I cry.

"Nothing," says the copyeditor, "I just added two little words to make it inclusive."

But I wasn't even thinking or talking "Inclusive"; I was clear up on the level of "Sexually Ignorant." Now gender has reared its ugly head in the midst of my simon-pure prose—although gender was the last thing in the world I wanted my reader thinking about. My sentence has been jerked down into the Level-4 language-game, whether or not that is where I wanted it. My pronoun now has been completely ruined; this was not simply the adding of an "or her." My "his" was sexually ignorant. Although still spelled the same, it is now a different word of precisely opposite function—anything but sexually ignorant.

And what about my representative individual? Do we now have a double image—an ideal female Christian alongside an ideal male Christian? (There is no doubt but that the feminist grammar does require sexual segregation where none is needed or called for.) But no, I don't think that is how the "his or her" pronoun is meant to operate. More probably it works like this: When the reader hits "his or her," he or she is to be reminded that he or she is a sexual creature, check it out real quick, and then choose the mental image that corresponds to his or her own sexuality. Now that is a cumbersome enough way of reading, to be sure; but the only alternative is the rejected one of letting us—at least for the nonce—forget all about sex (and feminism).

And who is actually more deserving of the charge of "sexism"? Me, for whom in such a case sex is the farthest thing from my mind, or the copy editor who proceeds to impose a sexual reference upon everything I write? Once more, of course, the feminist intent was innocent (comparatively). The aim was to make the language "inclusive," not force anthropology into an inherent dualism. But also once more, the accidental side effect has been to join the philosophy of the world in its Level-4 partitioning of the race.

CHAPTER SIX

The Eve of Adam (rather than The Dawn of Man)

NOW that we have developed the requisite language levels, we are ready to see that Genesis 1:27 is a mustard seed version of the great shrub of biblical anthropology:

> So God created man in his own image,
>   in the image of God he created him;
> Male and female he created them.

In summary, here are two levels of discourse: Level 1 with man as an indivisible integer, and Level 4 with mankind constituted of males and females. Both levels are true and both essential to a proper understanding of the passage. Yet even though both are necessary, the verse creates a clear priority between them. However, that priority is not here expressed in terms of chronology; only one act of creation is being described. Yet priority there most certainly is; the order of the two statements could not be reversed. Not only does the first statement come *first;* it is doubled for emphasis; and the "image of God" is ascribed to it alone. Man always is to be thought of as an undifferentiated unity before he is analyzed into constituents (of whatever sort). And although it is not explicit in this verse, we have seen that very quickly to be made explicit is the idea that, even on Level 4, the male and female constituents are to represent a molecular bonding rather than separated atoms. However the account is read, the *unity* of the race takes precedence over any of the *constituencies* of which it is composed.

THUS far the first creation account of Genesis 1:1–2:4a. However, many people have read the second, *narrative* account of 2:4b–25 quite differently. I want to argue that the two accounts can and should be read as speaking with one voice.

If the common understanding of the Genesis 2 story were put into Genesis 1 terminology (that in itself being a poor move) it would read something as follows: Now there is no creation of a Level-1, undifferentiated "man." And rather than creating them "male and female" in one action, God first created a *male* "in his image" and then later—as something of an afterthought, in a subordinate action—he created a female to go with the first-created male. (Be aware that Genesis 2 does not attribute an "image of God" to anyone—although people tend to correlate the two accounts just as we have done here.)

The question is whether there is a grammar that will even allow us to say what the preceding paragraph just undertook to say. Before the entrance of the female Eve into the story, it should be just as impossible to call Adam a "male" as it would be to speak or think of a "father" before there was a concept "child." There can't be a "father" without a "child"; no more can there be a "male" without a "female." To call the pre-Eve Adam a "male" actually is to get ahead of the story, to have moved into a language game that does not and cannot yet exist at that point.

It was Wittgenstein, again, who pointed out that language comes into being—and can come into being—only as a fruit of human experience. And in human experience there is nothing that properly could be called "male" except in relation to "female"; they exist together or not at all. Until there is Eve, Adam must be considered simply as an undifferentiated human being—undifferentiated sexually, racially, and in every other way. (And once more, people were playing WITTGENSTEIN before Ludwig came out with the game: there is an ancient Jewish tradition that this Adam was androgynus.) I prefer "undifferentiated"; but in any case, such an Adam stands as a very nice representation of Level-1 creation. God created *man* (not "a male") as a total, singular, personal unity.

Now hear that this does not mean (nor am I asking you to imagine) that this Adam was some sort of nonhuman monstrosity or that he underwent some sort of physiological transformation with the creation of Eve. Put it that, even before Eve, he was observed to have genitals of the sort we now call "male." There would then have been no way of knowing them to be *male* sex organs—or even *sex organs* for that matter. There would be no way of figuring out *why* they were formed as they were or what possible function they might have (they indeed having no function until there was Eve). Adam might even be observed to have sperm. But what is sperm? It certainly cannot be understood as an indication of *maleness* until one knows what the sperm itself is. And if one does not know and cannot know "ovum" (there being as yet no Eve), there is no chance of explaining "sperm." This Adam could have acted as he would; but he could not have been called "macho" or "lover" or much of anything else.

Most of our human attributes are *relational* and have no function and thus no identification apart from their complementary attribute.

Adam *became* "male" (*could* become "male") only in Eve's becoming "female." So, even in Genesis 2, it is not "first the male and only later the female." No, just as in Genesis 1, "male and female he created them." Before that moment, genitals, sperm, and all the rest added up to... nothing. Then suddenly, after that moment, "Oh! Her!... Why, of course... How could we have been so stupid? So that is why everything is as it is. Right on!" "Male *and* female" makes such very good sense; either one alone makes no sense at all.

So Genesis 2 turns out to be a very good *narrative* version of Genesis 1:27. And that parthenogenetic bit about Adam's rib being tickled into going female while the rest of him went male is a pretty neat way of affirming that "male and female he created them" is indeed the direct antiphon to "in the image of God he created him." And finally, Genesis 2 takes the prize in making so emphatic what 1:27 had missed, namely, the so very "molecular" design of human males and females.

CHAPTER SEVEN

God's Gender and Ours

HOWEVER, the argument developed here needs also to be applied at a higher level—indeed, at the highest possible level. It will work there—and with very interesting results.

If the concepts "male" and "female" *must* come into being simultaneously, if the words can enter the language only together, then it follows that *God* could become "masculine" only in that moment when *his* "rib" (God-imaged, Level-1 "man" of course) became "feminine." (We are replacing the word "male" with "masculine" so that we can speak of God's *gender* without ascribing to him anything like physical, biological *sexuality*.) But we mean exactly what we say and do now seriously intend to argue that the Bible presents the race itself as being essentially "feminine" in relation to the "masculinity" of God. Man is a woman— to put it in a way that is linguistically maddening and yet biblically true.

Biblical usage indicates that the God/man relationship is to be understood primarily under three figures— each of which casts God in a clearly masculine role: (a) husband and wife (or lover and beloved); (b) father and child (normally "children" or "son"); and (c) king and people (never, as I recall, king and an individual subject). The very terminology immediately commits us to "molecular" rather than "atomic" thought. God-with-man is meant to exist as a "marital molecule," a "family molecule," or a "royal molecule" (and a king cannot be king or be royal unless there is a people). In each case, the molecular implication of mutual sub-ordination is very much present. H_2O cannot exist as water without the hydrogen atoms and oxygen atoms each being willing to give up their right to independent existence as hydrogen or oxygen. And yes, God did subordinate himself in the creation of man and has continued to subordinate himself ever since—even to death on a cross. Yet, in each case, God is masculine—and must be for the figure to work.

At first glance, there might not seem to be any hint of a "God-with-man molecule" idea in the Genesis anthropology we have been examining; but that glance is wrong. Since in the second, narrative account (3:4) being "*like* God" is the serpent's line, the very phrase used to denote man's *negative* action of sin, disobedience, and *atomism*, then the first-account phrase "in the image of God" must intend something quite different from being "like God." What, then? Most obviously, this: To be "in the image of God" means to be in a *complementary* (not competitive) relationship to him, to be in *correspondence*. For God and man to "image" each other means that they are to be "co-respondents," each answering to the other, man's being the very hydrogen needed to combine with God's oxygen (with God, of course, also being the chemist in charge) if, together, they are to find their high destiny as WATER.

Obviously, to this day, the hydrogen has not responded very well; but that does not change the fact of what man was *created* to be. But as we already have seen, in human language "male and female" is perhaps our very best model of *personal* correspondence; hydrogen and oxygen atoms are hardly personal at all. So, if we reject all masculine language for God, how, pray tell, are we to do any effective exegesis of "created in the image of God"?

AN EXCURSUS ON THE UNITY OF GOD IN THE LANGUAGE OF CANAAN

IT regularly is argued that, although the masculine and feminine *together* certainly have always constituted the nature of God, the *cultural* biases and limitations of the era made it impossible fully to express that truth in scripture. Yet such a suggestion is just the opposite of the truth. In the religio-cultural world of Bible times, Yahwism (the worship of one God, the Old Testament Yahweh) was perhaps the only religion that did *not* have both the masculine and the feminine principle represented in deity—and these customarily in explicitly *sexual* pairings. In the chronological sequence of their impact upon biblical thought, the religions that included both male and female deities within their pantheons would be: the Sumerian, the Egyptian, the Canaanite, the Assyrian, the Babylonian, the Persian, the Greek (including the mystery cults), and the Roman.

The fact that most, if not all, of these cultures were even more strongly male dominated than was Israel shows that Israel's so-called "patriarchalism" certainly was no bar to attributing femininity to Yahweh. And the later Christian development of *trinitarian* doctrine shows that Israel's "monotheism" was no bar to feminizing God, either; multifacetedness and variety can be attributed to God without compromising his oneness. *Culturally*, at any time in its history, Israel could have come up with the concept which currently is being advanced among us, namely, a God incorporating equally the masculine and feminine in one Person. Indeed, what is culturally inexplicable is that, particularly under the pressures of Canaanite Baalism, Israel failed (or refused) to accept any hint or tinge of such dual-gendered deity.

Far from admitting *cultural* explanation, this anomaly calls for *theological* explanation. It is not that Yahwism denies any place or standing to the feminine; not at all. It is, rather, that Yahweh does not need or want a female consort, *because he already has one.* Man is that consort (already *is* in the sense that God loves us and has covenanted with us; *called to be* in the sense that we have yet to respond as the true and faithful consort). But Hosea was willing to go so far as to say that our greatest need is to "know" Yahweh, using at that point the very Hebrew term that also denotes sexual union. And most telling to me is the discovery—right in the middle of Jeremiah's famous "new covenant" passage (31:31–34)—of the completely casual, unsignaled phrase, "my covenant which they broke, though I was their husband." Obviously, Jeremiah's hearers didn't need any explanation. How else had they ever understood "covenant," how else *could* it be understood, except as the marriage between Husband Yahweh and Wife Israel? It is not wide the mark to say that, in Yahwism, the human race plays the role that goddesses play in the religions of dual-gendered deity.

This means that the biblical faith has built into it a much higher anthropology than is possible to any of the pagan faiths—and let it be said, an anthropology that not only fully *includes* women but actually is *biased toward* the feminine. Consequently, we ought to be very cautious about falling for the temptation our biblical predecessors so valiantly resisted, namely, moving the feminine principle into the godhead and thus jeopardizing the great anthropological (and feminist) advantage scripture had already given us.

YET even apart from the Genesis "image of God," when we look at the total biblical witness the gender implications of the God/man relationship become all the more explicit. The "Father/child" model is, of course, very pervasive. But also pervasive is the model of the male/female lovers. In the Old Testament, Yahweh/Israel as husband/wife (or wooer/wooed) is prominent. In the New Testament, Christ/church as bridegroom/bride is just as prominent. And in both cases, certainly, the model of what Israel or the church is to be is also the model of what the race itself should be.

However, to refuse to speak of God as masculine (out of whatever motives) is necessarily to lose these models and their understanding of the God/man relationship. It is *for our sakes* that God has deigned to reveal himself to us as "masculine," to aid us in becoming "feminine" in response. Yet we would reject that approach, choosing rather to treat him as "beyond gender." And why? The mentality of the age would indicate that we resent the intimacy and self-giving that "femininity" would require of us.

The rebuttal, of course, is that these models are only *analogies* or *metaphors* of God—with the implication that, consequently, they are to be understood sheerly as cultural creations which we do not need to take seriously, which we are free to exchange for imagery of our own choosing or to drop in favor of speaking directly of things in themselves. In this regard, however, it should be noted that the feminist grammar has not proposed any different models that come anywhere close to approximating the biblical ones.

Very true, these are "analogies"—but the adjective "only" does not follow. As Wittgenstein has told us, language is created solely out of *human* experience and is expressive solely of human experience. Further, as human beings, we are incapable of any direct, unmediated prehension of God. Therefore, whatever we say about God will *have* to be analogy. Indeed, Dorothy Sayers went so far as to suggest that all human speech is analogical and can't be any other way. Thus, discovering our models to be *analogical* cannot be made an excuse for dismissing them as *peripheral*. The masculinity of God is as thoroughly rooted in the totality of scripture as is any idea one could name. Of course, no one can presume to say who or what God in himself is. But if the Bible is taken as incorporating God's self-revelation in any sense, then it reveals that God wants us to relate to him as one who is "masculine personal." Whatever he may be in himself, *for us* he is Husband, Father, and King.

However, there is more that follows. Wittgenstein established that language grows out of human experience. That implies that all of our gender and sexual *terminology* has proceeded out of our human gender and sexual *experience*. But although that is undoubtedly true *linguistically*, it does not follow that the same order holds *theologically*. Biblically, "human sexuality" is not the first great fact of our existence (as the world would have it). Linguistically, yes, but theologically it is not true that God's gender is nothing more than a backward cultural projection of our own human sexuality. Quite the contrary, our human sexuality is itself an imperfect derivative of that perfect gender relationship established when the in-that-moment-becoming-masculine God created a feminine humanity in his own image. There is where we must look to see what it *really* means to be "male and female."

So it is not that the prophet Hosea pulled off an heroic act of marital fidelity and then presented that as a paradigm for understanding Yahweh's relationship to Israel. Rather, because Yahweh always had been the sort of husband he was to Israel, Hosea was inspired to act as he did toward Gomer. In Ephesians 5:25, Paul asks husbands to love their wives as Christ loved the church; he does not tell husbands to take note of how they treat their wives and from that learn how Christ loved the church. It is not our human ideas and experience that define true "masculinity" and "femininity"; we stand as very poor models of those. No, those are to be "read out of " the God/man relationship and accordingly "lived into" our experience as human males and females.

But when the feminist grammar would forbid us to think of God as masculine and thus know him as lover or father, this is not only to reject God in his chosen approach, the way *he* chose for revealing himself; it is also to rob ourselves of the one model by which there was any chance of our understanding our own sexuality and learning to use it for its intended purposes and blessings. Our refusing to address him according to his express preference may insult him, but it certainly cannot change or harm him. The irreparable harm comes to ourselves. Out of a distaste for distinguishing between the sexes in any way, for us to deny his *masculinity* inevitably is to deny the call that we be *feminine* in relation to him. And what hope is there that we ever can come to be "in the image of God" if we refuse to hear what that means?

AN EXCURSUS ON GENDER AND DEITY

WE have established that God has revealed himself to us as "masculine" precisely in order to invoke our (humanity's) "feminine" response—and we have no desire to back off on that point. However, we never meant to suggest that God is nothing but masculine, that "masculinity" can serve as his *total* characterization. No, if we may put it so, God equals "masculinity" plus "*deity*"—and those two are not the same thing. As masculine, he is *Father* (to us as *children*) and *Wooer-Husband* (to us as *beloved-bride*). But as divine, he is also *Deity* (to our *humanity*), *Lord* (to our *liege*), and *Creator* (to our *creature*).

However, to confuse God's masculinity with his deity is disastrous. As masculine, he is not only the object of humanity's feminine response; he is also the model of how human males should be masculine in relation to human females. Yet God's deity is no part of *that* package. His deity is without analogy at any level of interhuman relations. Some humans are indeed called to be father or wooer-husband to other humans. But no male (or female) is to be god to anyone else; the divine roles of lord and creator are unique to God. Recall that it was *the serpent* who suggested that man eat the fruit and become "like God" (in this sense); and that of course was a bad move that didn't work very well at all.

Yes, it is true that the male animal very often has *wanted* to make his masculinity toward the female include his being god over her. And in one sense contemporary feminism is correct in asserting that women have just as much right to play god as men do. Yet, biblically, this is a very poor way of putting the matter: there the word is that *no one* is right in wanting to be "like God," not that men and women should have equal rights in being so!

Granted, I have addressed only the linguistic matter of why the Bible's consistently masculine reference to God is proper, is theologically constructive, humanly helpful, and in no way threatening or disparaging to any segment of the race. I have not gone on to explore the specifics of what the masculine God's relationship to a feminine humanity has to say about the male-female relationships of human beings. In *this* book, we are trying to stick to the topic of "language." The broader topic, although admittedly crucial, must await later treatment.

YET another implication follows from what we have been saying. If "God created man in his own image" comes *before* "male and female he created them"; if "man" represents Level-1 discourse and "male and female" Level-4; and if "sexually undifferentiated Adam" stands prior to "male Adam and female Eve"—then it follows that a gender-undifferentiated God would outrank the masculinized one of the creation. So the feminists are right. Assuming that their "God beyond gender" is the equivalent of our "gender-undifferentiated God," theirs is a commendable effort to lift our God-talk to the highest possible level. Glory to God in the highest!

Theoretically that may be true—but it is also to forget *whose* is the language with which we are dealing, *who* are the speakers of it, and what is our own place in the scheme of things. Whoever or whatever God may have been before the creation, before he made us and addressed us, before he became masculine in relation to our femininity, surely it is not for us to make language claims there. After all, we are *of* the creation, *of* God's rib that became wife. How, then, do we presume to step out of that status to speak as definer and describer of the God that was before, to address him (it) as though *that* is God *pro nobis*, for *us*, to *us*, with *us*?

We can possibly know of God only as much as he has chosen to reveal of himself. And he has revealed himself to us only in, by, and through our own history, by way of that which is relevant to our own historical existence. He has addressed us only as his beloved, only as feminine co-respondent to his own masculinity, not as confidant to his existence before the worlds began. But we try to go God one better by approaching him on a level higher than the one he has assigned us. We think to *improve* upon Jesus' "Pray then like this: 'Our Father . . .'" (Mt. 6:9) or upon Paul's "When we cry, '*Abba*! Father!' it is the Spirit himself bearing witness with our spirit that we are children of God" (Rom. 8:15–16).

But this cannot pass as a human *honoring* of God. It is rather the *presumption* of the serpent's invitation to become "like God," of wanting to be *more* than he has made us to be and offering him *more* than he has asked of us. And the situation is even worse when we must suspect that the real interest in "the God beyond gender" is not that of speaking as truly of God as is possible but of evading the subordination attendant upon confessing him as husband or father or lord.

Again (and for the last time), I do not mean to suggest that the feminist grammar was *designed* with the intent of presuming against God and evading the self-abasement he rightfully requires of us. No, I think it represents, rather, the tunnel vision of zealotry—a quite thoughtless move to enhance the status of women without giving consideration to the consequences for theology and faith. It is not surprising that *secular* feminism should see no further and do no better. It is a great tragedy that *Christian* feminism got swept up in the process.

CHAPTER EIGHT

The End of the Matter

THE end of the matter is as Barth began it—that the gospel, the biblical message, *requires* the language of Canaan. That, of course, is not to suggest that it can be spoken only in Hebrew and Greek. It is to say that it must have a grammar powerful enough to enable us to think and say what the biblical languages were intent to communicate in the first place. And as seems clear, the grammar of contemporary humanism (whether feminist or otherwise) simply has not that capability. So unless we first go to the Bible for some language training, there is no chance of the gospel's being truly spoken or heard among us.

An Afterword

AFTERWARDS (i.e., after the events recounted in our Foreword and thus after the writing of this volume), Karl Barth's *The Christian Life*, a fragment-construction of Volume IV, Part 4, of his *Church Dogmatics* came to hand. And wouldn't you know, reading Barth opened my eyes to another prime characteristic, not simply of the feminist grammar, but more generally of the entire theological fashion of which the grammar is but a symptom.

What follows here is just one, early (p. 6), brief paragraph out of Barth's long- and many-paragraphed book. I intend someday to read the rest of it (a remark regularly found upon the lips of Barth-readers). Yet just this one paragraph is typical enough to make our point.

> Who is the *God* who commands in royal freedom? If we hold fast to God's self-declaration in Jesus Christ, then we may resolutely answer in the negative: he is not in any case a general or neutral god, however, lofty, who owes his closer definition to the intrinsically nonobligatory surmising or thinking of some human religion or metaphysics, even though it be that of the Christian faith. He is not in any case empty transcendence whose possible filling out can be provided only by human existence.

And we may no less resolutely answer in the positive: in any case, no matter how it may be with faith or unbelief, the obedience or disobedience of the man who confronts him, he is the one without whom this man would not even be. He is the one who has created him. No matter what many may think of it, God is the one who has reconciled man to himself when as a sinner man became his enemy. He is the one who in the concluding manifestation of his love wills to redeem man, and will redeem him from the discord in which he now exists. He is the partner of man as the Initiator and Lord of this history of his dealings with him. It is with him, with this one as outlined thus, that acting man comes to have and has dealings in that event of his encounter with God's command. The encounter is in any case determined and limited by the work and therefore by the manner of this Lord. It takes place in the sphere of the Father, the Son, and the Holy Spirit, who is man's Creator, Reconciler, and Redeemer.

(1) It is clearly the case that Barth's language can qualify only as what is regularly (if unfairly) called "sexist." It follows that Barth himself is guilty of "sexism," of ignoring and belittling women. His language is in no way "inclusive," in that he fails to make any specific reference to females or to use any specifically feminine pronouns or other such terminology.

(2) At the same time, it is obvious that any reader proficient enough in the English language (or the original German) to be reading Barth in the first place can understand this paragraph perfectly and know for certain that Barth is not discriminating against women—or anyone else. He properly uses generic terminology as a means of affirming that, in relation to

God (and thus on all major points of Christian theology), none of our human distinctions even merit notice. One and all, we are *human beings*, members of one race, each a full and equal participant in "man" and "men." There is not the slightest doubt but that this is what Barth has in mind; and any honest reader can know it for a fact. On the other hand, for Barth, at this point, to have said anything that would call attention to distinctions of gender, race, age, creed, piety, or anything else, at best would be to *detract* from the truth to which he was witnessing and at worst actually to *deny* it.

(3) If, as is done as a matter of course by many authors and editors, this paragraph had been written or edited to conform to feminist, "inclusive" usage— e.g., doubling nouns and pronouns to "women and men" and "he or she," changing "mankind" to "humankind," avoiding all pronouns in reference to God—this would be to make *trivial* Barth's whole effort. (I will now be using that word "trivial" with some frequency; upon it hinges the point I want to make.) The paragraph would no longer be *Karl Barth* speaking; it would no longer say what *he* wanted to say. He would no longer be speaking grandly upon his grand theme. He would have been preempted by trivial-mindedness.

But to try to make Karl Barth speak in inclusive language would be a lost cause in any case. Down the line a bit, because this particular volume happens to be structured over the Lord's Prayer, a chapter is devoted to a treatment of God as *Father*. (For *us*, that is, it would be a "chapter." On Barth's own scale, the entire volume is simply Chapter XVII and this merely a "section.") But therein (p. 51) he writes: "*Father* as a vocative, whether expressed or not, is the primal form of the thinking, the primal sound of the speaking, and the primal act of the obedience demanded of Christians."

Later (p. 53), he explains *why* "Father" is essential to our speaking of God and to God:

> Father! Understood as a vocative and used in Christian thought and speech, this word gives the required precision, the appropriate fullness, and the authentic interpretation to a word that in itself is indefinite, empty, and ambivalent, namely, the word "God." God himself, the one true and real God, obviously does not need this in order to avoid indistinctness, emptiness, and ambivalence. But the word "God" in all human languages does need it, for it can mean everything for some, this or that for others, and even nothing at all, or a mere illusion, for others."

Surely Barth himself never anticipated that there soon would be Christians who explicitly would *defy* God's command that he be invoked as "Father"; but he has put his finger on the heart of the matter even so. We are to see that much more is involved than simply an aversion to God's "masculinity." Quite beyond this specifically feminist concern, the theological bent of our day is toward moving God away from the specific and concrete and into what Barth calls "indistinctness, emptiness, and ambivalence"—and this, rather apparently, out of a desire to evade the specificities of God's judgment that many of our actions are "sins" and we ourselves "sinners," that there is One to whom we are subordinate, upon whom we are dependent, apart from whom we are nothing, in relation to whom we are to be self-forgetful, and in obedience to whom we must live or else in disobedience die. The questioning of God's "masculinity" is but a signal symptom of our deeper and more pervasive sickness.

So, Barth's language is irremediably sexist. Yet, Karl Barth being Karl Barth, I suppose most publishers would make an exception to their editorial rule and let his stuff through the way he wrote it. However, if the same manuscript bore the name of some lesser light (say, "Vernard Eller," whom many consider so lesser as to be no light at all), it might very well be rejected for its failure—or the author's refusal—to conform to the feminist usage. And this is trivial-mindedness.

Undoubtedly there are quarters of the theological world in which Barth's witness will not be read nor given consideration—merely because his language is found to be offensive. And that is a trivial-mindedness which spells nothing but the deprivation both of the potential reader and of contemporary theology.

(4) Barth's paragraph is entirely *biblical.* Its grammar is that of the Bible itself (whether in Hebrew, Greek, or English, as we have seen—and German in Barth's case). But more, each of Barth's ideas can be supported from scripture—and will be, with a small-print section, when Karl Barth is doing it.

(5) Even more, Barth's paragraph is *gospel.* In addition simply to having scriptural support, what he has to say reiterates the priority, emphasis, and inflection of the biblical gospel. What scripture makes basic (thus, that both "man" as a unity and "men" as every single individual are commanded by a God on whom they are utterly dependent), Barth makes basic. What

the gospel does not emphasize (thus, the priority of our sex roles and gender distinctions), Barth does not make central.

I am not arguing that Barth is infallible, above criticism, or a teacher of the only true theology. Personally, I have not even considered him as my own favorite, most essential theologian. Yet this much must be said: If "the Christian gospel" has any specific reference and a defineable content, and if the scriptures carry any authority in our locating that content, then Barth's paragraph and his theology as a whole are in the ballpark—something that definitely cannot be said about just every paragraph and every theology, and particularly those of current fashion. But the one thing of which Karl Barth will be the last to be accused is being trivial or of trivializing the gospel.

YET I can well imagine someone commenting upon our paradigmatic paragraph, "Dr. Barth, I must say that I found your words very offensive!"

To which I can also imagine Barth responding, "Yes, just so! It *is* offensive to learn that, before God, we all stand *together* to such an extent that he cannot and will not distinguish between the righteous and the unrighteous; between male chauvinist pigs and their innocent female victims; between a liberated, self-actualizing woman and her toadying, boot-licking counterpart; between humanity's heroic spirits and its unwashed philistines. It *is* offensive that God should be so blind as to ask us each to pray, 'Lord (and Father), be merciful to me, a *sinner*.' In fact, it is offensive that God should come on as 'Initiator and Lord,' suggesting that we are utterly dependent upon *him*, that human authenticity can be found only in our subordinating ourselves in obedience to *his* command. Yes, it *is* offensive—which is why the Rock of Offense himself said, 'Blessed is he or she who is not offended in me.'"

"But, Dr. Barth, that isn't what I meant! I didn't read that far—and I don't care about those things. I am offended that you talked about men and didn't once mention *women*—as though they don't even exist!"

"What? I didn't mention *women*? But I didn't say anything that *wasn't* about women—and everybody else. My dear sister, you didn't hear a word I said, did you? And you didn't really want to, did you?"

Could it be that, perhaps subconsciously, we use this trivial offense about the spelling of the language's generic terminology as a self-protective means of avoiding the *essential* offense with which the gospel would confront us?

I am not ready to go so far as to argue that a Barthian sort of in-the-ballpark presentation of the gospel absolutely *cannot* be stated in the grammar of feminism. However, I would opine that, wherever you *do* find literature being done in this grammar, it is odds-on that the theology involved *is* outside the ballpark, centering on what the gospel treats as secondary if not trivial. This is partly because the language does itself encourage such focus upon the human condition rather than upon God. It serves the situation that Christoph Blumhardt described even before Barth learned it from him:

> Everyone sighs over himself, looks for something in himself and for himself—and doesn't himself know what it is. One would like to call out to them all: "People, forget *yourselves*! Think of *God's cause*.

Start to do something for *it*. Don't be sorry for yourself; or at least be sorry that you have nothing to do but worry about your own petty concerns.

Yet our final word must accent what we have said before. Because this book is about *language*, we have focused there. However, we have not meant to suggest that the feminist grammar is itself the villain of the piece, that it has *caused* the shift away from an objective, Barthian-type, God-centered theology to a subjective, liberationist, human-centered one. Plainly, the theology has created the language rather than the other way around. The contrast between Barth's language and that of the feminists is but an indicator of the contrast between his theology and theirs. Yet this suggests that not even the feminist ideology is the *particular* villain. It is but one expression of today's trivialized theology that downplays the Father in an attempt to play up the children.

This book has stayed "little" by confining itself to the question of language. Yet it wants to be thought of as "big" (in the same sense though hardly to the extent of Barth) in that it treats the feminist grammar, not as an issue in itself, but as a means of exposing the smallness (triviality) of the human-locked world of and for which it would speak.